I0425845

May 2012

SECURITY FORCE ASSISTANCE

Additional Actions Needed to Guide Geographic Combatant Command and Service Efforts

GAO

Accountability ★ Integrity ★ Reliability

GAO
Accountability * Integrity * Reliability

Highlights

Highlights of GAO-12-556, a report to congressional committees

SECURITY FORCE ASSISTANCE

Additional Actions Needed to Guide Geographic Combatant Command and Service Efforts

Why GAO Did This Study

DOD is emphasizing security force assistance (e.g., efforts to train, equip, and advise partner nation forces) as a distinct activity to build the capacity and capability of partner nation forces. In anticipation of its growing importance, DOD has identified the need to strengthen and institutionalize security force assistance capabilities within its general purpose forces. Accordingly, a committee report accompanying the Fiscal Year 2012 National Defense Authorization Act directed GAO to report on DOD's plans. GAO evaluated: (1) the extent to which DOD has established its concept for conducting security force assistance, including defining the term and identifying actions needed to plan for and prepare forces to execute it; (2) the extent to which the geographic combatant commands have taken steps to plan for and conduct security force assistance, and what challenges, if any, they face; and (3) what steps the services have taken to organize and train general purpose forces capable of conducting security force assistance, and what challenges, if any, they face. GAO reviewed relevant documents, and interviewed officials from combatant commands, the services, and other DOD organizations.

What GAO Recommends

GAO recommends DOD clarify its intent for security force assistance, including how combatant commands should adjust their current planning efforts and provide a means to track activities. DOD partially concurred, stating that recent guidance addresses planning requirements. GAO continues to believe that more specific direction is needed.

View GAO-12-556. For more information, contact Sharon Pickup, (202) 512-9619, pickups@gao.gov.

What GAO Found

The Department of Defense (DOD) has taken steps to establish its concept for conducting security force assistance, including broadly defining the term and identifying actions needed to plan for and prepare forces to execute these activities. For example, in October 2010, the department issued an instruction that broadly defines security force assistance and outlines responsibilities for key stakeholders, including the geographic combatant commands and military services. DOD also identified gaps in key areas of doctrine, organization, and training related to the implementation of security force assistance and tasks needed to address those gaps. The tasks include reviewing joint and service-level doctrine to incorporate security force assistance as needed and developing measures to assess progress in partner nations. Citing a need to clarify the definition of security force assistance beyond the DOD Instruction, DOD published a document referred to as a Lexicon Framework in November 2011 that included information to describe how security force assistance relates to other existing terms, such as security cooperation.

The geographic combatant commands conduct activities to build partner nation capacity and capability, but face challenges planning for and tracking security force assistance as a distinct activity. Notwithstanding DOD's efforts to present security force assistance as a distinct and potentially expansive activity and clarify its terminology, the commands lack a common understanding of security force assistance, and therefore some were unclear as to what additional actions were needed to meet DOD's intent. Specifically, officials interviewed generally viewed it as a recharacterization of some existing activities, but had different interpretations of what types of activities should be considered security force assistance. Further, some command officials stated that they were not clear as to the intent of DOD's increased focus on security force assistance and whether any related adjustments should be made in their plans and scope or level of activities. As a result, they do not currently distinguish security force assistance from other security cooperation activities in their plans. DOD intended the Lexicon Framework to provide greater clarity on the meaning of security force assistance and its relationship to security cooperation and other related terms. However, some officials said that they found the distinctions to be confusing and others believed that additional guidance was needed. GAO's prior work on key practices for successful organizational transformations states the necessity to communicate clear objectives for what is to be achieved. Without additional clarification, the geographic combatant commands will continue to lack a common understanding, which may hinder the department's ability to meet its strategic goals. Moreover, the system that the commands are directed to use to track security force assistance activities does not include a specific data field to identify those activities. The commands also face challenges planning for and executing long-term, sustained security force assistance plans within existing statutory authorities, which contain some limitations on the types of activities that can be conducted.

The services are taking steps and investing resources to organize and train general purpose forces capable of conducting security force assistance based on current requirements. For example, to conduct activities with partner nation security forces, the Army and the Air Force are aligning certain units to geographic regions, and the Marine Corps has created tailored task forces. However, the services face certain challenges. Due to a lack of clarity on how DOD's increased emphasis on security force assistance will affect future requirements, they are uncertain whether their current efforts are sufficient or whether additional capabilities will be required. Further, services face challenges in tracking personnel with security force assistance training and experience, particularly in identifying the attributes to track.

_____ United States Government Accountability Office

Contents

Abbreviations List

DOD   Department of Defense
OSD   Office of the Secretary of Defense

May 10, 2012

Congressional Committees

In the past few years, the Department of Defense (DOD) has been emphasizing security force assistance as an important and distinct activity to build the capacity and capability of partner nation security forces in light of lessons learned from operations in Iraq and Afghanistan and counterterrorism operations with partner nations in other parts of the world. For example, the 2010 Quadrennial Defense Review generally described security force assistance as DOD's "hands on" efforts to train, equip, advise, and assist countries' forces in becoming more proficient at providing security to their populations, protecting their resources and territories, and enabling them to participate in operations that improve regional security, such as coalition and peacekeeping operations. Similarly, DOD's January 2012 Defense Strategic Guidance reiterated security force assistance as a key element of DOD's mission to counter terrorism, provide a stabilizing presence overseas, and share the costs and responsibilities of global leadership.[1]

While security force assistance is a recently introduced term within the department, the objective to develop the capabilities of partner nation security forces is not new and has traditionally been achieved through a broader set of activities and programs planned for and conducted by the geographic combatant commands, such as security cooperation,[2] security

---

[1]Department of Defense, *Sustaining U.S. Global Leadership: Priorities for 21st Century Defense* (Jan. 3, 2012).

[2]Security cooperation is defined as activities undertaken by DOD to encourage and enable international partners to work with the United States to achieve strategic objectives that includes all DOD interactions with foreign defense and security establishments that build defense and security relationships that promote specific U.S. security interests, develop allied and friendly military capabilities for self-defense and multinational operations, and provide service members with peacetime and contingency access to host nations.

assistance,[3] and foreign internal defense.[4] Historically, special operations forces have conducted the majority of DOD's activities to train, advise, and assist partner nation security forces, whereas the involvement of general purpose forces[5] has been more limited. As such, these forces had not been permanently organized and trained to carry out this mission. However, during operations in Iraq and Afghanistan, general purpose forces have been tasked with training and advising the security forces of those countries. Our prior work that was focused on U.S. efforts to advise and assist Iraqi and Afghan security forces observed challenges related to the way that ground forces were organized to conduct these missions.[6] In light of the experience in Iraq and Afghanistan and in anticipation of the growing role of security force assistance in U.S. strategy and future operations, the 2010 Quadrennial Defense Review identified the need to strengthen and institutionalize capabilities within the general purpose force to conduct security force assistance.

The House Armed Services Committee report accompanying the Fiscal Year 2012 National Defense Authorization Act bill (H.R. 1540) directed us to report on the department's plans to institutionalize security force assistance capabilities in the general purpose force.[7] To address this requirement, this report evaluates (1) the extent to which DOD has established its concept for conducting security force assistance, including defining the term and identifying actions needed to plan for and prepare

---

[3]Security assistance is a group of Title 22 programs authorized by the Foreign Assistance Act of 1961 and the Arms Export Control Act of 1976 or other related statutes by which the United States provides defense articles, military training, and other defense-related services by grant, loan, credit, or cash sales in furtherance of national policies and objectives.

[4]DOD Joint Publication 3-22 defines foreign internal defense as the participation by civilian and military agencies of a government in any of the action programs taken by another government or other designated organization to free and protect its society from subversion, lawlessness, insurgency, terrorism, and other threats to its security.

[5]General purpose forces are the regular armed forces of a country, other than nuclear forces and special operations forces, that are organized, trained, and equipped to perform a broad range of missions across the range of military operations.

[6]GAO, *Iraq and Afghanistan: Actions Needed to Enhance the Ability of Army Brigades to Support the Advising Mission*, GAO-11-760 (Washington, D.C.: Aug. 2, 2011) and *Iraq and Afghanistan: Availability of Forces, Equipment, and Infrastructure Should Be Considered in Developing U.S. Strategy and Plans*, GAO-09-380T (Washington, D.C.: Feb.12, 2009).

[7]H.R. Rep. No. 112-78, p. 112.

forces to execute security force assistance; (2) the extent to which the geographic combatant commands have taken steps to plan for and conduct security force assistance, and what challenges, if any, they face; and (3) what steps the services have taken to organize and train general purpose forces to be capable of conducting security force assistance, and what challenges, if any, they face.

To address these objectives, we reviewed DOD and service strategic guidance, policy, and doctrine related to security force assistance. We also examined the roles and responsibilities for security force assistance identified in DOD Instruction 5000.68 *Security Force Assistance* and the tasks identified through DOD's security force assistance capabilities-based assessment. Further, we reviewed documentation related to activities currently being conducted by the geographic combatant commands to engage with partner nation security forces and evaluated various military service efforts to organize and train forces capable of meeting current requirements from the geographic combatant commands to conduct such activities and address future requirements. Finally, we met with officials throughout the department and its components, including, but not limited to, the Assistant Secretary of Defense for Special Operations/Low-Intensity Conflict; the Joint Staff; Defense Security Cooperation Agency; military service headquarters, force providers, and training organizations; U.S. Special Operations Command; four of the six geographic combatant commands—U.S. Africa Command, U.S. Central Command, U.S. European Command, and U.S. Southern Command—and selected service component commands. In these discussions we corroborated the information provided in the documents above and discussed the commands' understanding of the security force assistance concept and steps being taken to implement it, and the development of relevant plans, requirements, and capabilities. We focused on the department's efforts to plan for and conduct security force assistance in areas of responsibility other than Afghanistan because DOD's focus on security force assistance is more long term than current operations in Afghanistan and the scope of the mission in that country may not be typical of efforts worldwide. In addition, while we understand the State Department is a critical stakeholder in U.S. security force assistance efforts, our review focused solely on DOD efforts to plan for and institutionalize security force assistance.

We conducted this performance audit from July 2011 to May 2012 in accordance with generally accepted government auditing standards. Those standards require that we plan and perform the audit to obtain sufficient, appropriate evidence to provide a reasonable basis for our findings and conclusions based on our audit objectives. We believe that the evidence obtained provides a reasonable basis for our findings and conclusions based on our audit objectives. Appendix I contains additional information about our scope and methodology.

Background

Range of DOD Efforts to Engage with Partner Nation Security Forces

DOD engages with partner nation security forces through a range of security cooperation efforts, which can include security assistance and foreign internal defense. Security cooperation is the broad term used to define those activities taken by DOD to build relationships that promote specified U.S. interests, build partner nation capabilities for self-defense and coalition operations, and provide U.S. forces with peacetime and contingency access. These activities are carried out under various statutory authorities. For example, DOD may conduct activities with partner nations, such as sending out military liaison teams, exchanging military personnel between units, and conducting seminars and conferences in theaters of operations under U.S. Code Title 10.[8] DOD also may conduct security cooperation activities through security assistance programs, authorized by U.S. Code Title 22,[9] which include foreign military sales and foreign military financing programs, and allow DOD to provide defense articles and services to partner nations in support of U.S. national policies and objectives. These security assistance programs are tools that can allow DOD to train and equip partner nation security forces. Additionally, the National Defense Authorization Act provides for authorities to facilitate DOD's engagement with partner nations under certain conditions.

DOD's 2010 Quadrennial Defense Review cites building the security capacity of partner nations as a key mission area and emphasizes security force assistance as an increasingly critical element of this mission. It also identifies several initiatives to enhance its ability to build partner nation security capacity, such as strengthening and institutionalizing general purpose force capabilities to conduct security

---

[8]See, for example, 10 U.S.C. 168.

[9]See, for example, 22 U.S.C. 2311 et seq. (Foreign Military Assistance) and 22 U.S.C. 2347 et seq. (International Military Education and Training).

force assistance; enhancing linguistic, regional, and cultural abilities; strengthening and expanding capabilities to train partner nation aviation forces; and strengthening the department's capacities for ministerial-level training. Historically, DOD has primarily relied on special operations forces to train and advise partner nation security forces as part of their foreign internal defense mission, which is to assist foreign governments in protecting themselves from internal threats. More recently, the increased demand on special operations forces in Iraq and Afghanistan has required the department to use general purpose forces to advise and assist the Iraqi and Afghan security forces. For example, in Iraq and Afghanistan, DOD has used training and transition teams and augmented brigade combat teams, respectively, to train, advise, equip, and mentor those countries' security forces. As a result of its experiences in Iraq and Afghanistan, its increasing emphasis on the importance of security force assistance, and its intent to expand these types of efforts to other parts of the globe, DOD has highlighted the need to further develop security force assistance capabilities within its general purpose forces.

Geographic Combatant Command Theater Campaign Plans Develop Strategies for Engaging with Partner Nations

To perform its military missions around the world, DOD operates six unified military geographic combatant commands, which are responsible for a variety of functions including planning for and conducting missions that range from humanitarian assistance to combat operations.[10] Each geographic combatant command is supported by service component commands (Army, Navy, Marine Corps, and Air Force) and a theater special operations command. In addition, the military services are responsible for organizing, training, and equipping their forces to execute the current and future operational requirements of the combatant commands.

As part of their planning responsibilities, geographic combatant commands develop theater campaign plans, which are multiyear plans that reflect the command's strategy to achieve certain end states within their areas of responsibility.[11] These plans are the primary vehicle for

---

[10]Current geographic combatant commands include U.S. Africa Command, U.S. Central Command, U.S. European Command, U.S. Northern Command, U.S. Pacific Command, and U.S. Southern Command.

[11]DOD defines the term "end state" to mean the set of required conditions that define achievement of the commander's objectives.

designing, organizing, integrating, and executing security cooperation activities. A hierarchy of national and strategic guidance—including the *National Security Strategy*, the *National Defense Strategy*, the *National Military Strategy*, and the *Guidance for Employment of the Force*—informs the development of the combatant commands' theater campaign plans. For example, the *Guidance for Employment of the Force* provides 2-year direction to geographic combatant commands on security cooperation, among other things, and consolidates and integrates DOD planning guidance related to operations and other military activities into a single overarching document. This guidance is considered essential to geographic combatant command planners as it provides the strategic end states that form the basis for theater campaign plans, including the assumptions and level of detail to be considered in developing those plans. For example, the *Guidance for Employment of the Force* has eight security cooperation focus areas, which include Operational Access and Global Freedom of Action, Operational Capacity and Capability Building, and Interoperability with U.S. Forces / Support to U.S. Capabilities. These focus areas are designed to link geographic combatant command security cooperation activities to achieve theater campaign plan end states. In order to execute the activities in their theater campaign plans, geographic combatant commands request the required force capabilities through the Global Force Management system. The Global Force Management system is a DOD system that provides insight into the global availability of U.S. military forces to meet rotational and emergent force requirements from geographic combatant commands as they arise.

DOD Has Taken Steps to Establish Its Concept for Conducting Security Force Assistance, Including Broadly Defining the Term and Identifying Actions Needed to Plan for and Prepare Forces to Execute It

DOD has taken steps to establish its concept for conducting security force assistance, including broadly defining the term and identifying actions needed to plan for and prepare forces to execute security force assistance activities. For example, DOD issued an instruction that broadly defines security force assistance and outlines responsibilities for key stakeholders. The department also conducted an assessment to identify gaps in key areas such as doctrine, organization, and training related to the implementation of security force assistance across the department. This effort identified tasks to address these gaps and called on DOD to develop a document, referred to as the Lexicon Framework, to clarify the term security force assistance and its relationship to other key terms.

DOD Has Issued an Instruction That Broadly Defines Security Force Assistance and Outlines Responsibilities for Key Stakeholders

In October 2010, DOD issued an instruction—DOD Instruction 5000.68—that broadly defines security force assistance and outlines responsibilities for key stakeholders to plan, prepare for, and execute security force assistance. The instruction defines security force assistance as "DOD activities that contribute to unified action by the U.S. government to support the development of the capacity and capability of partner nation forces and their supporting institutions."[12] The instruction states that DOD should develop and maintain forces, including general purpose forces and special operations forces, that can conduct security force assistance activities in a variety of conditions that include (1) politically sensitive environments where an overt U.S. presence is unacceptable to the host country government; (2) environments where a limited, overt U.S. presence is acceptable to the host country government; and (3) environments where a large-scale U.S. presence is considered necessary and acceptable by the host country government. According to Office of the Secretary of Defense (OSD) and U.S. Special Operations Command officials, special operations forces would be favored to lead missions in

---

[12]Department of Defense Instruction 5000.68, *Security Force Assistance* (Oct. 27, 2010).

the first environment, and the other environments could either use general purpose forces or an appropriate combination of forces. [13]

In addition, responsibilities of key stakeholders, including the geographic combatant commands and the military services, to plan for and conduct security force assistance are outlined in the instruction. For example, DOD Instruction 5000.68 states that the

- geographic combatant commands should incorporate security force assistance into their theater campaign plans; conduct security force assistance within their areas of responsibility; annually forecast and report security force assistance requirements for a 5-year time frame; and record security force assistance activities into the Theater Security Cooperation Management Information System; and

- military services should develop, maintain, and institutionalize capabilities to support DOD efforts to organize, train, equip, and advise foreign military forces and their supporting institutions; provide scalable capabilities to meet geographic combatant command requirements for security force assistance; develop training and education standards for security force assistance capabilities; and identify and track military service personnel who have security force assistance-related training, education, or experience.

DOD Has Identified Tasks to Address Gaps in Implementing Security Force Assistance and Developed a Lexicon Framework Intended to Clarify the Meaning of Security Force Assistance

DOD conducted a capabilities-based assessment to identify gaps in key areas of doctrine, organization, training, materiel, leadership and education, personnel, and facilities, related to the implementation of security force assistance across the department. The effort resulted in an April 2011 Joint Staff memorandum that identified 25 tasks needed to address the identified gaps, along with the organizations responsible for completing the tasks and associated milestones. [14] The tasks have targeted completion dates through April 2014 and include recommending changes to joint and service-level doctrine to incorporate security force assistance as needed; developing measures to assess security force

---

[13]Officials noted that special operations forces rarely operate without the support of general purpose forces, and therefore, general purpose forces would not be excluded from operating in any of the three environments.

[14]The Joint Staff, *Security Force Assistance DOTMLPF Change Recommendation*, Joint Requirements Oversight Council Memorandum 050-11 (Apr. 19, 2011).

assistance progress in partner nations; and developing joint training standards for U.S. forces training for security force assistance missions.

Citing a need to clarify the definition of security force assistance beyond the information found in DOD Instruction 5000.68, the Joint Staff memorandum also directed DOD to develop a lexicon framework. In November 2011, DOD published the Security Force Assistance Lexicon Framework. According to the Lexicon Framework, its intent was to promote a common understanding of security force assistance and related terms by providing greater clarity on the definition of security force assistance and how it relates to other existing terms, such as security cooperation and security assistance.[15] The Lexicon Framework also expands upon the DOD Instruction's definition of security force assistance. Specifically, DOD Instruction 5000.68 states that security force assistance is defined as "DOD activities that contribute to unified action by the U.S. government to support the development of the capacity and capability of partner nation forces and their supporting institutions." The Lexicon Framework restates this definition, but also adds that security force assistance is all DOD activities conducted under various programs to "organize, train, equip, rebuild/build, and advise foreign security forces and their supporting institutions from the tactical to ministerial levels."

DOD Has Established Organizations to Manage Its Efforts to Implement Security Force Assistance

DOD has established organizations to help manage its security force assistance implementation efforts. For example, in February 2011, the department established a Security Force Assistance Steering Committee and Working Group to guide the department's efforts to develop security force assistance policy and capabilities, and manage the implementation of DOD Instruction 5000.68 and the completion of the tasks noted in the Joint Staff memorandum. The Steering Committee and Working Group are both cochaired by Assistant Secretary of Defense for Special Operations/Low-Intensity Conflict and the Joint Staff J-5 Strategic Plans and Policy directorate, and also include other DOD organizations. For example, U.S. Special Operations Command and the military services are included in the steering committee, and the geographic combatant commands participate in the working group.

---

[15]Department of Defense, *Security Force Assistance Lexicon Framework* (Nov. 1, 2011).

Additionally, DOD established the Joint Center for International Security Force Assistance in 2006, which according to its charter is supposed to collect, analyze, and document security force assistance lessons learned and best practices, advise and assist the geographic combatant commands, the military services, and other government agencies with security force assistance, and actively support the long-term integration of security force assistance into joint training, leader development, and doctrine. This center is funded through the Army's training budget and received $1.3 million in base funding for fiscal year 2012 with the majority of this used to cover civilian personnel costs, as well as operating costs and travel costs for personnel. The center has focused on supporting the warfighter in Iraq and Afghanistan, but recently has begun to conduct outreach with geographic combatant command planners to educate key staff on security force assistance and how to incorporate it into theater campaign planning efforts. It previously published a Security Force Assistance Planner's Guide in 2008, most recently updated in 2009, and officials stated that the center is updating the Planner's Guide for 2012 in light of the generally accepted set of terms in the lexicon and to serve as a resource for planners of security force assistance.

The department also relies on other long-standing organizations to support U.S. efforts to interact with partner nation security forces. For example, the Defense Security Cooperation Agency is responsible for administering certain security cooperation and security assistance activities that fall under Title 10 and Title 22 of the U.S. Code. In addition, Defense Security Cooperation Agency officials said the agency offers opportunities to help educate personnel on ways to provide security cooperation assistance to partner nations. For example, the Defense Institute of Security Assistance Management, an institute run by the Defense Security Cooperation Agency, provides professional education, research, and support to enhance security assistance management capabilities of DOD military and civilian personnel. Moreover, Defense Security Cooperation Agency officials cited the Defense Institution Reform Initiative and the Ministry of Defense Advisors program as two efforts that were developed to help support geographic combatant command efforts to build capacity and capability of partner nations' ministerial institutions.

Geographic Combatant Commands Face Challenges That Limit Their Ability to Plan for and Track Security Force Assistance as a Distinct Activity

The geographic combatant commands are conducting activities to build partner nation capacity and capability, but face challenges planning for and conducting security force assistance as a distinct activity, including the following: (1) a lack of common understanding of security force assistance which may limit their ability to plan for it as OSD intends; (2) limitations in the system where security force assistance activities are to be tracked; and (3) the ability to develop and execute long-term security force assistance plans within existing legislative authorities.

Geographic Combatant Commands Lack a Common Understanding of Security Force Assistance

OSD has presented security force assistance as a distinct activity requiring the geographic combatant commands to develop new and innovative strategies that go beyond traditional security cooperation. However, despite DOD's effort to clarify its terminology, the four geographic combatant commands we spoke to lack a common understanding of security force assistance, and therefore some are unclear as to the additional efforts that may be needed on their part to meet the department's intent for security force assistance and do not see the value in distinguishing security force assistance from other security cooperation activities.

OSD Has Presented Security Force Assistance as a Distinct and Strategic Activity

According to officials from the Security Force Assistance Working Group, the emphasis recently placed on security force assistance in the Quadrennial Defense Review, Defense Strategic Guidance, and other documents like DOD Instruction 5000.68 and the Lexicon Framework, is indicative of DOD's intention to take a more strategic and proactive approach to building the capacity and capability of partners and allies around the world. DOD documents characterize security force assistance as a subset of security cooperation, but identify it as a distinct activity from other types of security cooperation activities. The Lexicon Framework states that the purposes of security force assistance are to create, maintain, or enhance a capacity or capability to achieve a desired end state. It distinguishes these purposes from other types of security cooperation activities, such as activities conducted to gain access, influence, or diplomatic or political action with a partner nation, but do not enhance any capacity or capability. To further illustrate this distinction, an OSD official said that the geographic combatant commands conduct security cooperation activities, such as military-to-military engagements and joint exercises, but these activities do not have the primary purpose to build partner nation capacity and capability and thus are not considered security force assistance. The Lexicon Framework states that the effective execution of security force assistance requires geographic combatant commands to develop objectives for the development of partner nation security forces, articulate regional objectives, link resources to overarching goals, and create operational roadmaps for persistent cooperation. It further states that this comprehensive, global approach to improving partner security capacity will require new and innovative strategies and authorities that go beyond traditional security cooperation applications.

According to OSD, the emphasis on security force assistance in recent guidance reflects an expectation that geographic combatant commands will conduct increased security force assistance activities through sustained and proactive plans focused on building partner nation capacity and capability. For example, Security Force Assistance Working Group officials said that as U.S. forces are drawn down in Afghanistan, the demand for security force assistance outside of Afghanistan is expected to increase over the next few years. The geographic combatant commands are expected to identify and plan for security force assistance based on the needs of the partner nations in their areas of responsibility and forecast the forces needed to conduct planned activities. The services, in turn, are responsible for providing forces to meet the geographic combatant commands' forecasted requirements.

Geographic Combatant Commands Lack a Common Understanding of Security Force Assistance and View It as a Recharacterization of Some Existing Security Cooperation Efforts

DOD Instruction 5000.68 directs the geographic combatant commands to incorporate security force assistance into their theater campaign plans and to forecast their force requirements for security force assistance. Notwithstanding DOD's efforts to present security force assistance as a distinct and potentially expansive activity beyond existing security cooperation efforts, geographic combatant commands lack a common understanding of security force assistance, and therefore some are unclear as to the additional efforts that may be needed on their part to meet the department's intent for security force assistance and do not see the value in distinguishing security force assistance from other security cooperation activities. Generally, all four of the geographic combatant commands we spoke to viewed security force assistance as a recharacterization of some of their existing security cooperation activities since all of the commands conducted some activities, such as training partner nation forces, targeted to build partner nation capacity and capability. The lack of common understanding of security force assistance both among and within geographic combatant commands led to inconsistencies regarding which of their current activities they considered to be security force assistance when discussing their efforts, including the following:

- Officials from one service component command told us that they consider nearly every activity with partner nations to be security force assistance—from subject matter expert exchanges that are meant to increase interoperability between the nations to U.S. instructor-led training of partner nation security forces—because they believe them to build the capacity and capability of partner nations.

- U.S. European Command identified individual efforts to train partner nations as security force assistance, such as its efforts to train infantry battalions from the country of Georgia to deploy to Afghanistan, but excluded activities such as military-to-military exchanges.

- U.S. Africa Command considered only comprehensive, persistent programs to improve partner nation security forces from the tactical to the ministerial to be security force assistance and identified only one activity as such. However, officials from one of the command's service components identified episodic activities aimed at increasing regional and maritime safety and security within the command's area of responsibility as security force assistance.

In addition, the geographic combatant commands we visited plan for interactions with partner nations, including some activities to build partner nation capacity and capability. However, because the geographic combatant commands view security force assistance as a recharacterization of some of their existing security cooperation activities, they did not see a need to distinguish security force assistance from other security cooperation activities in their planning efforts, as indicated in the following examples:

- U.S. European Command officials said that they did not incorporate the term security force assistance in their theater campaign plan, but the plan emphasizes the importance of building allies' and partners' capacity to contribute to regional security.

- U.S. Southern Command's theater campaign plan includes one specific reference to security force assistance, but includes references to other activities that link back to the command's military objectives, including objectives related to building partner capacity and capability.

- U.S. Africa Command's theater campaign plan includes some general references to security force assistance, but the references are not linked to specific objectives. The plan does include information on the need to develop partner nation capacity and capability.

- U.S. Central Command officials said they do not use the term security force assistance in their theater campaign plan.

Further, some geographic combatant command officials said that they were not clear as to OSD's intent behind the emphasis on security force assistance, including the level of effort that should be devoted to it, and whether that intent should have any effect on their future theater plans and activities. Officials from several combatant commands said that they develop their theater campaign plans and strategies based on the *Guidance for Employment of the Force* and other strategic guidance and that they would expect any emphasis requiring them to change how they plan for and conduct activities to be reflected in that guidance. According to OSD, strategic guidance documents are being reviewed to determine whether they should be revised based on the January 2012 Defense Strategic Guidance to reflect greater emphasis on security force assistance.

We recognize that the department has taken steps intended to increase understanding of security force assistance, such as the issuance of the Lexicon Framework in November 2011. Nonetheless, as the above examples demonstrate, the geographic combatant commands continue to lack a common understanding of security force assistance, what additional efforts may be needed on their part to meet the department's intent for security force assistance, and the value of distinguishing security force assistance from other security cooperation activities. We also recognize that the Lexicon Framework was issued recently. However, some geographic combatant command and service officials familiar with the framework said that they found some of the distinctions within the document to be confusing and others cited the need for additional guidance that provides greater clarity on what is required to plan for and conduct security force assistance as OSD intends. Further, officials from the Joint Center for International Security Force Assistance said that, while they believe the Lexicon Framework is helpful to clarify the relationship between security force assistance and other related terms, joint doctrine on security force assistance is necessary to ensure that all stakeholders understand security force assistance. Moreover, we found that neither the framework nor the instruction provide clear guidance on the level of effort that geographic combatant commands should devote to security force assistance and how security force assistance differs from some of the geographic combatant commands' current efforts to build partner nation capacity and capability. Our prior work on key practices for successful organizational transformations shows the necessity to communicate clear objectives for what is to be achieved.[16] Further, DOD guidance states that clear strategic guidance and frequent interaction between senior leaders and planners promotes an early, shared understanding of the complex operational problem presented, and of strategic and military end states, objectives, and missions.[17] Without additional clarification from OSD, the geographic combatant commands will continue to lack a common understanding of security force assistance, which may hinder the department in meeting its strategic goals.

System for Tracking Security Force Assistance Activities Contains Limitations

DOD Instruction 5000.68 directs the geographic combatant commands to record their security force assistance activities in the Theater Security Cooperation Management Information System, which, according to officials, has been identified by the *Guidance for Employment of the Force* as the system of record for tracking all security cooperation activities. Beyond the challenges that commands face in distinguishing between security force assistance activities and other types of activities, we also found that the system into which they are instructed to track security force assistance activities has limitations. For example, the system does not contain a corresponding data field specifically for security force assistance activities. There are several different versions of the Theater Security Cooperation Management Information System currently in use by the geographic combatant commands and service component commands, including individual command legacy systems and an interim system being used by multiple commands. According to a Joint Staff official, neither the interim version of the Theater Security Cooperation Management Information System nor the legacy systems, with the exception of the system put in place by the Army, contain a data field for specifically tracking security force assistance activities. The Joint Staff is currently developing the Global Theater Security Cooperation Management Information System to replace the legacy and interim systems in order to create a single global interface for users, with initial

---

[16]GAO, *Highlights of a GAO Forum, Mergers and Transformation: Lessons Learned for a Department of Homeland Security and other Federal Agencies*, GAO-03-293SP (Washington, D.C.: Nov. 14, 2002).

[17]Department of Defense, Joint Publication 5-0, *Joint Operation Planning* (Aug. 11, 2011).

fielding planned for fiscal year 2013. Joint Staff officials responsible for the development of this system told us no plans currently exist to create such a data field within the Global Theater Security Cooperation Management Information System. According to these officials, they are not planning to add this field because they believe security force assistance is a broad category and different users of the system may prefer more specific data fields for the individual types of engagements with partner nations, such as military-to-military engagement and training. Security Force Assistance Working Group officials have suggested that a security force assistance field should be added to the Global Theater Security Cooperation Management Information System because tracking and monitoring security force assistance activities is important to ensure that the department is directing resources toward its strategic goal of building partner capacity and capability. As the department continues to develop and manage security force assistance as a stand-alone concept, without a data field or other mechanism within the future Global Theater Security Cooperation Management Information System to specify which activities are security force assistance activities, and a consistent approach to collecting data on these activities, OSD will lack visibility over both security force assistance activities and the U.S. resources being invested in building the capacity and capability of partner nations.

Moreover, while the Theater Security Cooperation Management Information System is intended to enable planning, tracking, and forecasting security cooperation activities, eliminate potential overlap and duplication of activities by different commands, and ensure that resources are being directed towards priority countries, the different versions of the system currently lack standard global business rules to guide how information on activities should be entered. Thus, it is up to the geographic combatant commands and services to develop their own set of rules—formal or informal—governing how activities are entered into the legacy and interim systems. Some commands enter all proposed activities into the system, while another enters data less consistently thus reducing the value of the system as a planning and forecasting tool. The inconsistency of reporting in this system can result in an inefficient use of resources. For instance, Navy officials told us of a recent example in which an Air Force-sponsored medical engagement with a partner nation was conducted in the same location as a similar Navy-sponsored medical engagement, but the Air Force was unaware of this until it arrived on location. The officials noted that, had the activities been identified and forecasted in the system, the Air Force and Navy could have coordinated and either chosen to redirect resources to another location or planned the activities to build upon one another. As part of the process to update the

Global Theater Security Cooperation Management Information System, Joint Staff officials recognize the need to have some level of standardization in how activities are entered across the department so that they have a complete and consistent picture of global activities, and are in the process of developing global business rules to that effect, expected to be completed by the end of fiscal year 2012.

Geographic Combatant Commands May Face Challenges in Developing and Executing Long-Term Security Force Assistance Plans within Existing Statutory Authorities

Geographic combatant commands conduct security cooperation and security assistance activities, which may include security force assistance, through a variety of different statutory authorities within Title 10 (Armed Services) and Title 22 (Foreign Relations and Intercourse) of the U.S. Code. For example, geographic combatant commands conduct security cooperation activities including military-to-military engagements, interoperability activities, and joint training exercises under traditional Title 10 authorities. DOD also can conduct activities involving interactions with partner nation security forces through State Department-led Title 22 security assistance programs and authorities, which include, foreign military sales, foreign military financing, international military training and education, and peacekeeping operations. All of the geographic combatant commands we spoke with told us that they used Title 22 programs such as Foreign Military Assistance[18] and International Military Education and Training[19] to provide training to partner nation forces. While the statutory authorities codified within Title 10 or Title 22 remain available unless Congress repeals them, other authorities are temporary and must be renewed periodically through legislation. For example, the annual National Defense Authorization Acts can provide specific authorities that allow the geographic combatant commands to conduct activities, such as counternarcotics training with partner nations. Table 1 below shows selected statutory authorities used by geographic combatant commands to conduct security cooperation and security force assistance activities.

---

[18]22 U.S.C. 2311 et seq.

[19]22 U.S.C. 2347 et seq.

Table 1: Select Statutory Authorities

Statutory authorities	Description
Military-to-Military Contacts and Comparable Activities (10 U.S.C. §168)	Authorizes combatant commands to conduct and fund military to military contacts with foreign country defense establishments and military forces, to include: traveling contact teams, military liaison teams, exchanges of military personnel between units, seminars and conferences held in theater of operations, and distribution of publications in theater of operations. Funds may not be used for the provision of defense articles or defense services to any country or for international military education and training.
Foreign Military Sales/Financing, Arms Export Control Act of 1976, as amended (22 U.S.C. §2761, 2762, 2769 and 22 U.S.C. 2673)	Authorizes government-to-government sales of U.S. defense articles, services, and training, including professional military education and technical training related to equipment purchases to foreign countries. Additionally, allows financing for the acquisition of U.S. defense articles, services, and training by allied and friendly nations through grants.
International Military Education and Training, Foreign Assistance Act of 1961, as amended (22 U.S.C. §2347 et seq.)	Authorizes military education and training to military and related civilian personnel of foreign countries to (1) further regional stability through mutually beneficial military-to-military relations; (2) provide training that augments the capabilities of partner nations' military forces to support combined operations and interoperability with U.S. forces; and (3) increase the ability of foreign military and civilian personnel to instill and maintain basic democratic values and protect internationally recognized human rights in their own government.
Peacekeeping Operations (22 U.S.C. §2348)	Authorizes assistance to friendly countries, on such terms and conditions as the President may determine, for peacekeeping operations and other programs carried out in furtherance of the national security interests of the United States.
Counter Drug Training Support, National Defense Authorization Act of Fiscal Year 1991 (Pub L. No.101-510), Section 1004	Authorizes counternarcotics-related training of foreign military and law enforcement personnel conducted by both special operations and general purpose forces for light infantry, aviation, coastal, riverine, rotary wing operations, and staffs associated with counterdrug operations. Counterdrug support can only be only used with selected countries. This authority was extended through fiscal year 2014 by Pub. L. No. 112-81, sec. 1005.
Global Train and Equip, National Defense Authorization Act of Fiscal Year 2006, Section 1206 (Pub. L. No. 109-163)	Authorizes Secretary of Defense to provide training, equipment, and supplies to partner nations in order for that country to conduct (1) counterterrorist operations or (2) participate in or support military and stability operations in which U.S. armed forces are a participant. Funding is annually authorized and appropriated by Congress. Funding cannot be provided directly to partner nation and cannot be used to directly support Afghan security forces, lift partner nation troops or equipment to theater, loan equipment, train or equip non-Ministry of Defense forces, or pay for construction. This authority has been amended multiple times and was extended through fiscal year 2013 by Pub. L. No. 112-81, sec. 1204(c).
Global Security Contingency Fund, National Defense Authorization Act of Fiscal Year 2012, Section 1207 (Pub. L. No. 112-81)	Authorizes a fund to be available to the Secretary of Defense or the Secretary of State to provide assistance to foreign countries to (1) enhance the capabilities of a country's national military forces, and other national security forces that conduct border and maritime security, internal defense, counterterrorism operations, and associated government agencies that support those forces; and (2) provide assistance for the justice sector, including law enforcement and prisons, rule of law programs and stabilization efforts in a foreign country. This authority expires at the end of fiscal year 2015.

Source: GAO.

These statutory authorities are specific in nature and some contain limitations and restrictions on the types of activities that can be conducted under these authorities. For example, the authorities codified within Title 10 do not authorize general purpose forces to conduct security force assistance activities, such as training, advising, and assisting partner nation security forces.[20] Thus, geographic combatant commands rely on statutory authorities beyond traditional Title 10 authorities, such as the aforementioned specific authorities provided for in the National Defense Authorization Acts or through Title 22 security assistance programs. For example, both U.S. Central Command and U.S. Southern Command stated that they used authority originally provided by section 1004 of the Fiscal Year 1991 National Defense Authorization Act to conduct counterdrug and counternarcotics training with militaries in their respective regions. Further, all four of the geographic combatant commands that we spoke to had at some point used authority originally provided by section 1206 of the Fiscal Year 2006 National Defense Authorization Act to train and equip partner nation forces. Like Title 10, many of these National Defense Authorization Act authorities and Title 22 security assistance programs have limitations in how they can be used. For example, section 1206 of the Fiscal Year 2006 National Defense Authorization Act only allows for training and equipping programs that build the capacity of foreign militaries to conduct counterterrorism operations or participate in or support military and stability operations in which U.S. forces participate.[21]

Once the geographic combatant commands' theater campaign plans are approved by the Secretary of Defense, they must find separate authorization for activities that they will conduct with partner nations. Some geographic combatant command and service component command officials said that they often have to cobble together multiple authorities in order to carry out a single activity with partner nation forces because of the specificity of the authorities. For example, officials from one service component command stated that a single training event targeted toward building the aviation capabilities of a partner nation required 11 different authorities and funding streams.

Some geographic combatant command officials noted that they may require additional or revised authorities in order to plan for and conduct

---

[20]See, for example, 10 U.S.C. 168.

[21]Pub. L. No. 109-163, sec. 1206(a)(1) as amended by Pub. L. No. 110-417, sec. 1206(a)(1)(A) and Pub. L. No. 112-81, sec. 1204.

GAO-12-556 Security Force Assistance

increased and sustained security force assistance activities, such as training and equipping partner nation forces, beyond their current level of effort. According to an OSD official, current authorities generally allow for more short-term relationships with partner nations, but planning for and conducting security force assistance as the department envisions it requires longer-term, sustained interaction. In that regard, this official stated that the department has efforts underway to review the current statutory authorities available to DOD to determine whether additional authorities are needed and to potentially develop proposals to Congress. As of February 2012, DOD was still conducting this review.

The Services Are Developing General Purpose Forces with Capabilities to Conduct Security Force Assistance to Meet Current Requirements but Lack Clarity on Future Requirements

The services are taking steps and investing resources to organize and train general purpose forces that are capable of conducting security force assistance and tracking uniformed military personnel with related experience and training. However, the services' efforts are still in progress and uncertainties remain about any additional capabilities that may be needed due to a lack of clarity in regard to future geographic combatant command requirements.

The Services Have Taken Some Steps and Invested Resources to Organize Dedicated Forces

DOD Instruction 5000.68 directs the services to develop, maintain, and institutionalize the capabilities to support DOD efforts to organize, train, equip, and advise foreign military forces and relevant supporting institutions in order to meet the geographic combatant command requirements. In providing these capabilities, it further elaborates that the services are to meet the requirements of all three conditions identified by the instruction under which security force assistance activities are conducted, and to identify joint capabilities across all domains, such as air, land, maritime, and cyberspace. The services have historically built teams on an as-needed basis to engage with partner nation security forces rather than developing dedicated forces to conduct these activities. However, officials stated that lessons learned from Iraq and Afghanistan established the need to organize and deploy forces to train and advise partner nation security forces in a more deliberate manner. In light of this experience, and the department's growing emphasis on security force assistance, the services have undertaken efforts to organize dedicated forces that they consider to be capable of conducting security force assistance. For example, service efforts include the following:

- The Army is planning to regionally align forces that will be tailored to meet the requirements of the geographic combatant command to which they are aligned. The regionally-aligned forces will remain at homestation and deploy only those elements of the unit that are required to meet the specific geographic combatant command requirements. The Army's initial regionally-aligned force will be a brigade combat team that will be aligned to U.S. Africa Command starting in January 2013, with additional forces expected to be aligned to the other geographic combatant commands beginning in fiscal year 2014. Although the initial unit will be a brigade combat team, officials said that future aligned forces could be smaller or larger units, depending on geographic combatant command requirements and can be augmented by specialized capabilities as needed. This initial regionally-aligned brigade is to conduct approximately 120 activities with partner nations within U.S. Africa Command's area of responsibility over the course of a year. According to Army headquarters officials, most of the 120 activities will be short-duration, small-footprint activities, conducted by teams as small as three people, while larger exercises with partner nations may be longer duration events, conducted by battalion-sized units.

  The aligned brigade will receive training for the full spectrum of operations,[22] comprising offense, defense, and stability operations, as well as tailored language, culture, and advising training for the specific missions. The Army has identified language proficiency as a beneficial skill but is still determining the level of language proficiency required within its regionally-aligned forces. For the initial regionally-aligned brigade, the Army plans to provide the majority of the brigade with basic language training that would allow it to build rapport with partner nation security forces, while smaller elements of the brigade are intended to receive more specialized training in one of the five key languages identified for Africa: Arabic, French, Swahili, Hausa, or Portuguese. In addition, a small portion of the brigade may be sent

---

[22]According to Army officials, based on guidance from the Chief of Staff of the Army, the latest doctrine uses the term "decisive action" to refer to full-spectrum operations.

through a full culturally-based language training course provided by a language training detachment at the unit's homestation. After the initial regional alignment, the Army will assess the level of language training that was provided to see whether it is sufficient or whether it should be adjusted for future regionally-aligned forces.

Once fully established, the Army's regionally-aligned forces are expected to conduct most engagements with partner nation security forces, but officials stated that the Army will still employ other options as necessary to meet combatant command requirements. The Army is projecting costs of approximately $1 million to establish the aforementioned language training detachment. In addition, the Army is estimating costs of about $100,000 for soldiers to travel to train with the 162nd Infantry Brigade. Army headquarters officials told us that the costs for force generation of the initial regionally-aligned brigade are not expected to be substantially different than those for a standard infantry brigade being trained for full-spectrum operations.

- The Marine Corps has organized several types of forces to meet geographic combatant command requirements with deployed teams ranging in size from one or two marines to larger task forces. For example, the Marine Corps deploys tailored special-purpose marine-air-ground task forces on a rotational basis to different regions to conduct activities with partner nation security forces. These task forces are meant to build military capacity of partner nations, provide regional stability, and develop lasting partnerships with nations in the region. According to officials, the Marine Corps also has small teams, such as 15-to-50-person security cooperation teams to conduct military-to-military engagements, and 11-person coordination, liaison, and assessment teams that have specific cultural knowledge of regions and are available to help the Marine Corps component commands with planning, coordination with partner nation forces, and assessment of partner nation forces. In addition to these efforts, the Marine Corps has been conducting a sustained effort with the country of Georgia's military, called the Georgia Deployment Program, to train and deploy Georgian battalions for full-spectrum operations in Afghanistan.

- According to officials, the Navy builds partner nation capacity and capability through a variety of ways using both its fleet and expeditionary forces. For example, officials stated that personnel from Navy ships regularly interact with partner nation security forces through port visits and engagements with partner nation navies.

Further, the Navy conducts ship-based rotational deployments, referred to as Partnership Stations, which include activities with partner nation security forces such as military-to-military engagements, exercises, and training. In addition to naval personnel, partnership stations also can include embarked marines or mobile training teams from other services depending on the activities planned by the respective geographic combatant commands. Moreover, the Navy provides expeditionary capabilities through its Naval Expeditionary Combat Command and Maritime Civil Affairs and Security Training Command. Specifically, the Maritime Civil Affairs and Security Training Command, budgeted in the Navy base budget to cost approximately $41 million for fiscal year 2012, is organized to provide tailored mobile training teams, referred to as Security Force Assistance Detachments, to geographic combatant commands to conduct training with partner nation navies across a range of topics such as small boat operations, weapons training, and leadership and professional development.

- The Air Force is standing up two mobility support advisory squadrons with one to be aligned to U.S. Africa Command and the other to U.S. Southern Command for the purposes of conducting capacity- and capability-building activities with partner nations. Mobility support advisory squadrons are expected to conduct activities in air mobility processes, such as maintenance, air traffic control, and airfield operations. All airmen assigned to the mobility support advisory squadrons receive training that is tailored to the region to which the squadron will be aligned. The mobility support advisory squadrons will remain at homestation and deploy only elements of the unit for specific activities as required to meet specific geographic combatant command requirements. Officials from Air Force Mobility Command stated that the approximate cost of standing up each squadron is just over $2 million, which covers the organizing, training, and equipping costs for the squadrons annually, but not the man-hours for the personnel in the squadrons. In addition to the mobility support advisory squadrons, the Air Force provides capabilities through mobile training teams and Extended Training Service Specialist teams,[23] among others.

---

[23]According to the Air Force Air Advising Operating Concept, Extended Training Service Specialists are permanent change of station teams that are technically qualified to provide advice, instruction, and training in the installation, operation, and maintenance of weapons, equipment, and systems.

As previously discussed, the department's emphasis on security force assistance is indicative of its expectation that the geographic combatant commands will conduct more security force assistance activities, such as organizing, training, and advising partner nation security forces to build their capacity and capability, and officials stated that they expect requirements for forces capable of conducting security force assistance activities outside of Afghanistan to increase in the future. The services' efforts to develop capabilities are based on the current requirements from geographic combatant commands, but without greater clarity in regard to future requirements, service officials stated that they are not able to assess whether their current efforts to develop force capabilities in this area are sufficient or whether additional capabilities may be required. For example, an Army official stated that the initial regionally-aligned force will provide the Army valuable information in regard to the sufficiency of the force to meet geographic combatant command requirements, the effectiveness of the training provided for the security force assistance mission, and the level of language proficiency required, but that future geographic combatant command requirements would influence the scope of the Army's efforts to develop capabilities for this mission. Additionally, Air Force officials said that the Air Force Campaign Support Plan is intended to provide structure and guidance to Air Force theater planners to support the development of future geographic combatant command security cooperation requirements, including security force assistance, which will then inform the Air Force's efforts to develop security force assistance capabilities.

Services Are Training Certain Personnel for Security Force Assistance, but Have Not Yet Fully Determined the Level of Training Required for All Security Force Assistance Activities

DOD Instruction 5000.68 directs the services to establish training and education requirements for personnel conducting security force assistance activities and to develop service-specific training and education proficiency standards for security force assistance capabilities. Training is a standard part of predeployment preparations for the formally organized units, such as the Army's regionally-aligned forces, the Air Force's mobility support advisory squadrons, the Navy's security force assistance detachments, or the Marine Corps special-purpose marine-air-ground task forces, and most of the services have established schools or organizations that provide language, culture, and advising training to these forces, as identified below:

- The Army provides some language, culture, and advising training through the 162nd Infantry Brigade located at Fort Polk, which was originally stood up to train forces for advise and assist missions in Iraq and Afghanistan. The 162nd is primarily focused on training advisors deploying to Afghanistan and will also assume the mission to train the Army's regionally-aligned brigade. As such, this organization receives funding from both the Army's base budget and overseas contingency operations funds[24] at a cost of $40.1 million for fiscal year 2012. The 162nd also can provide training to other Army teams that will engage with partner nation security forces at the request of unit commanders.

- The Marine Corps provides tailored language, culture, and advising training through the Marine Corps Security Cooperation Group. This group, budgeted to cost about $3.1 million[25] in fiscal year 2012, provides training to the Marine Corps' special-purpose marine-air-ground task forces and security cooperation teams, among others.

- The Air Force provides language, culture, and advising training through the Air Advisor Academy, which was initially stood up to train airmen deploying to Iraq and Afghanistan as advisors. According to Air Force headquarters officials, the Air Advisor Academy will provide training for up to 1,500 airmen in fiscal year 2013, including advisors deploying to Afghanistan, mobility support advisory squadrons, mobile training teams, and extended training service specialist teams, among others. The total cost for the Air Advisor Academy for fiscal year 2012 is expected to be approximately $6.4 million.

- The Navy provides its forces with language and culture training prior to every deployment, but has not established specific advisor training. According to Navy headquarters officials, because sailors typically deploy on ships for extended periods of time, the service trains them for a broad range of missions in accordance with the Fleet Readiness Training Program and based on the requirements set forth by the geographic combatant commands. As a result, Navy officials said that they would need clear security force assistance requirements from the geographic combatant commands to train forces to meet those specific requirements. Unlike the other services, the Navy's method for training depends less on training at schools and more on learning required skills from superiors while on the job. Officials added that,

---

[24]Overseas contingency operations funds are funds that support Operation Enduring Freedom, which focuses principally on Afghanistan, but also include operations in the Horn of Africa, the Philippines, and elsewhere.

[25]According to officials, of this approximately $3.1 million, 72 percent goes towards training and advising, 17 percent towards supplies, and 11 percent towards travel.

GAO-12-556 Security Force Assistance

since sailors can train their subordinates, they can also deliver subject-matter training to partner nation security forces, if necessary. However, expeditionary personnel assigned to the Maritime Civil Affairs and Security Training Command may receive training in methods of instruction and in the course topics they will be teaching while deployed.

Further, DOD and service officials noted that theater security cooperation planners' courses are available to personnel who may assist or be responsible for the geographic combatant command and service component command planning efforts. According to these officials, these courses are intended to provide an understanding of security cooperation planning, including some information related to security force assistance. For example, Marine Corps officials told us that the Marine Corps offers the Security Cooperation Planner's Course, which is a 1-week course that provides students with basic knowledge regarding security cooperation planning systems and operations, as well as the statutory authorities that allow for activities with partner nation security forces. Over the past 2 years, officials said that this course has been offered to a variety of organizations, including personnel from all of the military services, OSD, the Defense Security Cooperation Agency, and State Department. Additionally, according to Air Force officials, the Air Force has recently established an online course intended to provide Air Force planners and air advisors education and training in the areas of irregular warfare, security cooperation, security force assistance, and theater campaign planning, among other topics, and is developing a 1-week in-residence course at the Air Advisor Academy, projected to begin in September 2012.

However, while personnel complete predeployment training prior to deploying on missions, and the services have established the various training and education efforts discussed above, the services have not yet fully determined what level of training should be provided for forces deploying on an as-needed basis for shorter-term missions, such as for mobile training teams or for teams of individuals formed and deployed to conduct individual activities. The Air Force is in the process of developing an instruction that identifies which airmen will get training from the Air Advisor Academy and for which missions, and officials said that, at a minimum, the instruction will likely direct that all security force assistance missions will require some air advisor training. An Army headquarters official stated that it is difficult to determine which missions should require advisor training for the purposes of establishing an official requirement. For example, regionally-aligned forces deploying for months at a time to provide training to partner nation forces in Africa and a team of four individuals from Army Training and Doctrine Command deploying to conduct a 1-week classroom training could both potentially be considered security force assistance, but training and mission requirements could be significantly different, and it is unclear whether the latter would really require training on advising, language, and culture skills. Moreover, the Army has established security force assistance mission essential tasks and incorporated them into their mission essential tasks for full-spectrum operations. Similarly, the Marine Corps has published a security cooperation training and readiness manual, which includes training tasks required for personnel deploying on security cooperation missions, including security force assistance. Army and Marine Corps officials stated that personnel who do not attend the formal training provided by the 162nd Infantry Brigade and the Marine Corps Security Cooperation Group are still expected to be trained for those tasks based on unit commanders' analysis of the mission.

Services Have Taken Steps to Track Uniformed Military Personnel with Security Force Assistance Training and Experience, but Face Challenges Identifying What Should Be Tracked

DOD Instruction 5000.68 also directs the services to identify and track individuals who have completed security force assistance-related training, education, or experience in the Defense Readiness Reporting System with a relevant skill-designator indicating their security force assistance qualifications. The services are taking steps to approach this requirement in a variety of ways, including the following:

- The Army has established eight different Personnel Development Skill Identifiers that it believes are related to security force assistance, including an identifier for uniformed military personnel who have completed certain advisor training, such as that provided by the 162nd Infantry Brigade. These identifiers are self-reported or reported by unit commands to Army Human Resources Command and are recorded on each individual soldier's personnel record. In addition to identifying personnel through these identifiers, Army headquarters officials stated that they can identify individuals who have completed certain security force assistance deployments through existing personnel systems, such as deployments as advisors to Iraq and Afghanistan. As a result, these officials believe that the Army's current efforts to track individuals for security force assistance are sufficient until new requirements are determined by the geographic combatant commands or OSD.

- The Marine Corps has a database to track uniformed military personnel training and experience and will eventually be using that to track security force assistance and irregular warfare skills in accordance with those identified in the Chairman of the Joint Chiefs Instruction 3210.06 on irregular warfare.[26] According to both OSD and service officials, irregular warfare skills would include those skills needed to conduct security force assistance. Marine Corps officials stated that the Marine Corps is still evaluating different options of tracking deployment experience for security force assistance missions and has not yet identified how it will track skills related to advising.

- The Navy has personnel systems that would allow them to track security force assistance training and experience—to include qualification designators, Navy enlisted classifications, subspecialty codes, and community designators—but is not currently so. According to Navy officials, greater clarity is needed from OSD on what skills should be tracked and officials further stated that it is difficult to identify and track individuals who may conduct some security force assistance activities as part of a fleet rotation. For example, a sailor may conduct a single activity with a partner nation navy while aboard a ship, but it is not clear whether that experience merits tracking.

- The Air Force plans to track uniformed military personnel with security force assistance training and experience within its Career Path Tool database as part of its broader effort to track irregular warfare capabilities, in accordance with the aforementioned instruction on irregular warfare. Air Force headquarters officials said that they are not tracking personnel yet because the system has to be updated to allow for such tracking.

As noted above, the services are taking steps to track uniformed military personnel, but service officials have cited general challenges with regard to tracking, such as how best to capture the varying degrees of experience individuals may have in conducting security force assistance (e.g., a 2-week mission training partner nation security forces in Africa versus a year-long deployment as an advisor in Afghanistan). OSD Personnel and Readiness and the services are currently working together as part of the Security Force Assistance Working Group to discuss what types of skills, training, and experience should be tracked and in what

---

[26]Chairman of the Joint Chiefs of Staff Instruction 3210.06, *Irregular Warfare* (June 10, 2010). This Instruction identifies a baseline list of irregular warfare-relevant skills and experiences that will be tracked by services through existing personnel reporting systems.

systems, but these efforts are still in progress. Moreover, OSD Personnel and Readiness, in coordination with the services, is working to finalize a DOD Instruction that will define the process for tracking irregular warfare and security force assistance skills. According to officials, the instruction is expected to be completed before the end of fiscal year 2012.

Conclusions

Security force assistance has become an increasingly important and distinct element of U.S. military strategy, both in Afghanistan and elsewhere in the world, as the United States seeks to enable partner nations to assist in countering terrorism and establishing and maintaining regional security. In anticipation of its growing importance, DOD has taken steps intended to define and institutionalize the security force assistance concept throughout the department. We recognize this concept is still evolving, but the challenges we have identified suggest that additional clarification is necessary to better position stakeholders to plan for and prepare forces to execute security force assistance activities to meet the department's strategic goals. DOD needs to do more to define its intent for security force assistance, including the level of effort that geographic combatant commands should devote to security force assistance, how that intent should influence the geographic combatant commands' strategies, and what additional actions are required by the geographic combatant commands to plan for and conduct security force assistance beyond their existing security cooperation efforts. This clarification, along with an increased ability to track security force assistance activities, would facilitate the geographic combatant commands' planning efforts and would increase DOD's visibility over security force assistance efforts to ensure that resources are being directed toward identified strategic goals and measure progress in implementing various initiatives. Furthermore, these steps would inform the services' efforts to ensure that the capabilities that they are developing and thus, the resources that they are investing, are appropriate and adequate to meet future security force assistance requirements.

Recommendations for Executive Action

To instill a common understanding of security force assistance throughout DOD and therefore better guide the geographic combatant commands' and services' efforts to plan for and prepare forces to execute security force assistance, we recommend that the Secretary of Defense, in consultation with the Chairman of the Joint Chiefs of Staff, direct the Assistant Secretary of Defense for Special Operations/Low Intensity Conflict and the Chief of Staff, Joint Staff J-5, in their positions as cochairs of the Security Force Assistance Steering Committee, to develop or modify existing guidance that further defines the department's intent for security force assistance and what additional actions are required by the geographic combatant commands to plan for and conduct security force assistance beyond their existing security cooperation efforts. For example, DOD could include more-specific direction as to how to determine which activities should be considered security force assistance, how they should be discussed in plans, and whether an increased level of effort, such as increased scope, nature, or frequency of activities, is required.

To facilitate the management and oversight of resources being directed toward building partner capacity and capability, we recommend that the Secretary of Defense, in consultation with the Chairman of the Joint Chiefs of Staff, take actions to ensure that updates to the Global Theater Security Cooperation Management Information System and the business rules being developed provide a mechanism and guidance to stakeholders to specifically identify and track security force assistance activities.

Agency Comments and Our Evaluation

In written comments on a draft of this report, DOD partially concurred with our two recommendations, adding that it believes that the department has taken some steps that it believes address some of the issues identified in our report. The full text of DOD's written comments is reprinted in appendix II. DOD also provided technical comments, which were incorporated as appropriate.

DOD partially concurred with our recommendation that the Secretary of Defense, in consultation with the Chairman of the Joint Chiefs of Staff, direct the Assistant Secretary of Defense for Special Operations/Low Intensity Conflict and the Chief of Staff, Joint Staff J-5, in their positions as cochairs of the Security Force Assistance Steering Committee, to develop or modify existing guidance that further defines the department's intent for security force assistance and what additional actions are required by the geographic combatant commands to plan for and conduct security force assistance beyond their existing security cooperation efforts. In its comments, DOD stated that additional guidance to the geographic combatant commands and services would be useful to promote understanding of security force assistance. However, the department believes that recently published strategic and planning guidance incorporates security force assistance planning requirements. Specifically, it noted that the recently released Strategic Guidance, *Sustaining U.S. Global Leadership: Priorities for 21st Century Defense* emphasizes the importance of security force assistance planning and execution. Further, DOD stated that the recently released Theater Campaign Planning Planner's Handbook provides additional direction to the geographic combatant commands to incorporate security force assistance into campaign planning. DOD added that it will review other existing guidance for necessary modifications, as required.

We recognized in our report that DOD has issued various documents that emphasize the importance of building partner nation capacity and capability through security force assistance activities. Notwithstanding this guidance, we found that the geographic combatant commands continued to lack a common understanding of security force assistance, what additional efforts may be needed on their part to meet the department's intent for security force assistance, and the value of distinguishing security force assistance from other security cooperation activities. While we agree that the Defense Strategic Guidance emphasizes the importance of security force assistance in broad terms, it does not specify the level of effort that the geographic combatant commands should devote to security force assistance or how the emphasis on security force assistance should influence the geographic combatant commands' strategies. Further, we note that the handbook that DOD cited focused on theater campaign planning in general and does not specifically address planning for security force assistance as a distinct activity. Therefore, we continue to believe that more specific guidance is necessary.

DOD partially concurred with our recommendation that the Chairman of the Joint Chiefs of Staff direct the Joint Staff to ensure that updates to the Global Theater Security Cooperation Management Information System and the business rules being developed provide a mechanism and guidance to stakeholders to specifically identify and track security force assistance activities. The department stated that the Global Theater Security Cooperation Management Information System will be an important tool in identifying and tracking security force assistance activities. While DOD concurred that the global system and the business rules being developed should provide a mechanism to specifically identify and track these activities, it did not agree that it is the responsibility of the Chairman of the Joint Chiefs of Staff to direct this. Instead, DOD noted that a Governance Council, chaired by members from the Deputy Assistant Secretary of Defense for Partnership Strategy and Stability Operations, the Joint Staff J-5, and the Joint Staff J-8, maintains oversight and management of the system. In light of DOD's comments, we have modified our recommendation to reflect both Office of the Secretary of

Defense and the Joint Staff's shared role in overseeing the development of this system.

We are sending copies of this report to appropriate congressional committees, the Secretary of Defense, the Chairman of the Joint Chiefs of Staff, the Secretaries of the Army, Navy, and Air Force, and the Commandant of the Marine Corps. The report also is available at no charge on the GAO website at http://www.gao.gov.

If you or your staff have any questions about this report, please contact me at (202) 512-9619 or pickups@gao.gov. Contact points for our Offices of Congressional Relations and Public Affairs may be found on the last page of this report. GAO staff who made major contributions to this report are listed in appendix III.

Sharon L. Pickup
Sharon Pickup
Director, Defense Capabilities and Management

List of Committees

The Honorable Carl Levin
Chairman
The Honorable John McCain
Ranking Member
Committee on Armed Services
United States Senate

The Honorable Daniel K. Inouye
Chairman
The Honorable Thad Cochran
Ranking Member
Subcommittee on Defense
Committee on Appropriations
United States Senate

The Honorable Howard P. "Buck" McKeon
Chairman
The Honorable Adam Smith
Ranking Member
Committee on Armed Services
House of Representatives

The Honorable C.W. Bill Young
Chairman
The Honorable Norman D. Dicks
Ranking Member
Subcommittee on Defense
Committee on Appropriations
House of Representatives

Appendix I: Scope and Methodology

To determine the extent that the Department of Defense (DOD) has established its concept for conducting security force assistance, including defining the term and identifying actions needed to plan for and prepare forces to execute security force assistance, we reviewed relevant existing DOD doctrine, policy, and guidance, including the DOD Instruction 5000.68 Security Force Assistance. We also examined the Joint Requirements Oversight Council Security Force Assistance Change Recommendation Memorandum, which identified actions to be taken and organizations of primary responsibility and support to implement security force assistance across the doctrine, organization, training, materiel, leadership and education, personnel and facilities spectrum. Additionally, we reviewed the department's Security Force Assistance Lexicon Framework document to understand the department's attempt to further explain and clarify the security force assistance concept. We also met with officials from the Assistant Secretary of Defense for Special Operations/Low-Intensity Conflict, Office of the Under Secretary of Defense for Personnel and Readiness, the Joint Staff J-5 Strategic Plans and Policy directorate, and Joint Staff J-7 Operational Plans and Force Development directorate to discuss the security force assistance concept, its definition, the roles and responsibilities of stakeholders identified in the DOD Instruction and the Joint Staff Security Force Assistance Change Recommendation Memorandum, and what other steps the department has taken to implement the security force assistance concept. In addition, we met with Joint Center for International Security Force Assistance and U.S. Special Operations Command officials to discuss their understanding of security force assistance and role in the department's efforts to institutionalize the concept. Further, we examined the charter for the Security Force Assistance Steering Committee and Working Group, which the Assistant Secretary of Defense for Special Operations/Low-Intensity Conflict and Joint Staff J-5 cochair, to determine the group's responsibilities to implement and oversee security force assistance efforts throughout the department.

To identify the extent to which the geographic combatant commands have taken steps to plan for and conduct security force assistance, and what challenges, if any, they face, we met with officials from U.S. Africa Command, U.S. Central Command, U.S. European Command, and U.S. Southern Command and selected military service component commands. In these meetings, we discussed their understanding of the security force assistance concept, their responsibilities as outlined in the DOD Instruction, as well as their efforts to plan for, request forces for, and track theater security cooperation activities. These commands were selected and visited as a nonprobability sample of four of the six geographic combatant commands. U.S. Africa Command and U.S. Southern Command and their service component commands were selected because the Office of the Secretary of Defense (OSD) suggested them as primary examples of geographic combatant commands conducting security force assistance in a peacetime environment—the expected environment of future security force assistance efforts. The two other commands—U.S. Central Command and U.S. European Command and their service component commands—were selected because of efficiencies gained by colocation to other site visits. We examined relevant geographic combatant command and service component command planning documentation, such as theater campaign plans and strategy briefings related to theater security cooperation planning, requirements, and activities being conducted in their respective areas of responsibility. We further met with geographic combatant command and Joint Staff J-5 Strategic Plans and Policy officials regarding the Theater Security Cooperation Management Information System to discuss how the system is intended to be used, and reviewed documentation related to its development. Finally, we reviewed relevant statutory authorities and Defense Security Cooperation Agency and geographic combatant command guidance documents outlining available statutory authorities to determine the authorities and funding available for the execution of security force assistance, and discussed these authorities and related challenges with geographic combatant command and service component command officials.

To identify what steps the services have taken to organize and train general purpose forces to be capable of conducting security force assistance, and what challenges, if any, they face, we met with officials from the U.S. Army, U.S. Marine Corps, U.S. Navy, and U.S. Air Force who were responsible for implementing security force assistance within each service, including officials from each service's headquarters, force providers and training commands, and other service organizations related to security force assistance. We examined relevant service-level documentation, which included doctrine, policy and guidance, briefings, and white papers related to security force assistance. We also discussed with each service their efforts to implement the security force assistance concept, their understanding of the concept, service capabilities being developed, and any potential cost factors related to security force assistance. To understand how the services are organizing for security force assistance and what capabilities are being provided, we met with officials from the service headquarters and service force providers, including U.S. Army Forces Command, U.S. Marine Forces Command, U.S. Fleet Forces Command, U.S. Air Force Combat Command, and U.S.

Air Force Mobility Command. To understand the training and education that is being provided to service personnel who conduct security force assistance missions, we met with officials about service-level training and education from the U.S. Army 162nd Infantry Brigade, U.S. Marine Corps Security Cooperation Group, and the U.S. Air Force Air Advisor Academy, and discussed joint training standards with U.S. Special Operations Command. In addition, we met with service officials to discuss each service's efforts to track uniformed military personnel with security force assistance-related skills, training, or experience. We also met with the Office of the Under Secretary of Defense for Personnel and Readiness to discuss DOD efforts to establish policy and guidance for tracking uniformed military personnel with security force assistance skills, training, and experience departmentwide.

We interviewed the following organizations during our review:

- Office of the Assistant Secretary of Defense for Special Operations/Low-Intensity Conflict, Arlington, Va.
- Office of the Deputy Undersecretary of Defense for Personnel and Readiness, Arlington, Va.
- Office of Secretary of Defense Cost Assessment and Program Evaluation, Arlington, Va.
- Security Cooperation Reform Task Force, Arlington, Va.
- Joint Staff, Operations (J-3), Arlington, Va.
- Joint Staff, Chief of Strategic Plans and Policy (J-5), Arlington, Va.
- Joint Staff, Chief of Joint Exercises and Training Division (J-7), Arlington, Va.
- Defense Security Cooperation Agency, Arlington, Va.
- Joint Center for International Security Force Assistance, Fort Leavenworth, Kans.
- Unified and Geographic Combatant Commands

    - U.S. Africa Command, Stuttgart, Germany
    - U.S. Central Command, Tampa, Fla.
    - U.S. European Command, Stuttgart, Germany
    - U.S. Southern Command, Miami, Fla.
    - U.S. Special Operations Command, Tampa, Fla.

- Service and Unified Component Commands

    - U.S. Army Africa Command, Vicenza, Italy
    - U.S. Army European Command, Heidelberg, Germany
    - U.S. Army South, Fort Sam Houston, Tex.
    - U.S. Marine Corps Forces Africa, Stuttgart, Germany
    - U.S. Marine Corps Forces Central Command, Tampa, Fla.

- U.S. Marine Corps Forces Europe, Stuttgart, Germany
- U.S. Marine Corps Forces South, Miami, Fla.
- U.S. Naval Forces Africa, Naples, Italy
- U.S. Naval Forces Europe, Naples, Italy
- U.S. Naval Forces Southern Command, Mayport, Fla.
- U.S. Air Force Africa, Ramstein, Germany
- U.S. Air Force Europe, Ramstein, Germany
- U.S. Air Force South, Tucson, Ariz.
- Special Operations Command Central, Tampa, Fla.
- Special Operations Command Europe, Stuttgart, Germany
- Special Operations Command South, Miami, Fla.

- U.S. Army

  - Department of the Army, Military Operations-Security and Stability Office, Arlington, Va.
  - Army Security Force Assistance Proponent Office, Fort Leavenworth, Kans.
  - U.S. Army Forces Command, Fort Bragg, N.C.
  - Security Assistance Training Management Organization, Fort Bragg, N.C.
  - 162nd Infantry Training Brigade, Fort Polk, La.

- U.S. Marine Corps

  - Headquarters Marine Corps, International Affairs Branch, Arlington, Va.
  - Marine Corps Security Cooperation Group, Virginia Beach, Va.
  - Marine Forces Command, Norfolk, Va.
  - Center for Irregular Warfare Integration Division, Quantico, Va.

- U.S. Navy

  - Naval Operations N52 and N523, Arlington, Va.
  - U.S. Fleet Forces Command, Norfolk, Va.
  - Naval Expeditionary Combat Command, Virginia Beach, Va.
  - Maritime Civil Affairs and Security Training Command, Virginia Beach, Va.
  - Naval Education and Training Command, Pensacola, Fla.
  - Naval Education and Training Security Assistance Field Activity, Pensacola, Fla.

- U.S. Air Force

  - Headquarters, U.S. Air Force, Irregular Warfare Integration, Arlington, Va.
  - Headquarters, U.S. Air Force, Secretary of the Air Force International Affairs, Arlington, Va.

- Air Combat Command, Langley, Va.
- Air Mobility Command, Scott Air Force Base, Ill.
- Air Education and Training Command, Randolph Air Force Base, Tex.

We focused on the department's efforts to plan for and conduct security force assistance in areas of operation other than Afghanistan because DOD's focus on security force assistance is more long term than current operations in Afghanistan and the scope of the mission in that country may not be typical of efforts worldwide. Finally, we understand the State Department is a critical stakeholder in U.S. security force assistance efforts, but our review focused solely on DOD efforts to plan for and institutionalize security force assistance within the general purpose force.

We conducted this performance audit from July 2011 to May 2012 in accordance with generally accepted government auditing standards. Those standards require that we plan and perform the audit to obtain sufficient, appropriate evidence to provide a reasonable basis for our findings and conclusions based on our audit objectives. We believe that the evidence obtained provides a reasonable basis for our findings and conclusions based on our audit objectives.

Appendix II: Comments from the Department of Defense

OFFICE OF THE ASSISTANT SECRETARY OF DEFENSE
2500 DEFENSE PENTAGON
WASHINGTON, D.C. 20301-2500

SPECIAL OPERATIONS/
LOW-INTENSITY CONFLICT

APR 2 7 2012

Ms. Sharon L. Pickup
Director, Defense Capabilities and Management
U.S. Government Accountability Office
441 G Street, N.W.
Washington, DC 20548

Ms. Pickup,

This is the Department of Defense (DoD) response to the GAO draft report, GAO-12-556, "SECURITY FORCE ASSISTANCE: Additional Actions Needed to Guide Geographic Combatant Commands and Service Efforts," dated March 30, 2012 (GAO Code 351634).

The Department agrees with recommendation one that additional guidance to the Geographic Combatant Commands and to the Services would be useful to promote understanding of security force assistance. However, the Department believes that recently published strategic and planning guidance does incorporate security force assistance planning requirements. Further planning guidance will be published, as required.

The Department agrees with recommendation two that the Global Theater Security Cooperation Management Information System (Global – TSCMIS) will be an important tool to identify and track security force assistance activities. Upgrades and business rules for Global – TSCMIS will be developed through the Governance Council representatives and not solely by the Joint Staff as recommended in the draft GAO report.

The complete Department of Defense response to the recommendations accompanies this letter.

The Department appreciates the opportunity to comment on this draft report. Please direct any questions or comments you may have to Mr. Jim Coffman, at (703) 697-0738 and james.coffman@osd.mil.

Garry P. Reid
Deputy Assistant Secretary of Defense
Special Operations and Combating Terrorism

GAO DRAFT REPORT DATED MARCH 30, 2012
GAO-12-556 (GAO CODE 351634)

"SECURITY FORCE ASSISTANCE: ADDITIONAL ACTIONS NEEDED
TO GUIDE GEOGRAPHIC COMBATANT COMMAND AND
SERVICE EFFORTS"

DEPARTMENT OF DEFENSE COMMENTS
TO THE GAO RECOMMENDATIONS

RECOMMENDATION 1: The GAO recommends that the Secretary of Defense, in consultation with the Chairman of the Joint Chiefs of Staff, direct the Assistant Secretary of Defense for Special Operations/Low Intensity Conflict and the Chief of Staff, Joint Staff J-5, in their positions as co-chairs of the Security Force Assistance Steering Committee, to develop or modify existing guidance that further defines the department's intent for security force assistance and what additional actions are required by the geographic combatant commands to plan for and conduct security force assistance beyond their existing security cooperation efforts.

DoD RESPONSE: DoD partially concurs. The Department's recently released Strategic Guidance, *Sustaining U.S. Global Leadership: Priorities for 21st Century Defense*, emphasizes the importance of security force assistance planning and execution. In addition, the recently released Theater Campaign Planning Planner's Handbook provides additional direction to the geographic combatant commands to incorporate security force assistance into campaign planning. The Department will review other existing guidance for necessary modifications, as required.

RECOMMENDATION 2: The GAO recommends that the Chairman of the Joint Chiefs of Staff direct the Joint Staff to ensure that updates to the Global Theater Security Cooperation Management Information System and the business rules being developed provide a mechanism and guidance to stakeholders to specifically identify and track security force assistance activities.

DoD RESPONSE: DoD partially concurs. DoD concurs that the Global Theater Security Cooperation Management Information System (Global-TSCMIS) and the business rules being developed provide a mechanism and guidance to stakeholders to specifically identify and track security force assistance activities. DoD non-concurs that it is the responsibility of the Chairman of the Joint Chiefs of Staff to direct that action. Global-TSCMIS oversight and management is accomplished through a tri-chair Governance Council led by the Deputy Assistant Secretary of

2

Defense for Partnership Strategy and Stability Operations, the Joint Staff J-5 Deputy Director for Partnership Strategy, and the Joint Staff J8 (South), Deputy Director for Command, Control, Communications, and Computers (C4). The council membership is comprised of an advisory member group made up of stakeholders from across the Department. It is the responsibility of this group to decide on all development and proposed changes to the Global-TSCMIS Governance Council. As the Council Administrator charged with scheduling, coordination, and agenda preparation, the Joint Staff J-5 Partnership Strategy representative will present this topic for consideration in a future Governance Council Meeting.

Appendix III: GAO Contact and Staff Acknowledgments

GAO Contact

Sharon Pickup, (202) 512-9619 or pickups@gao.gov

Staff Acknowledgments

In addition to the contact named above, James A. Reynolds, Assistant Director; Grace Coleman; Mark Dowling; Kasea Hamar; Ashley Lipton; Charles Perdue; Michael Pose; and John Van Schaik made key contributions to this report.

GAO's Mission	The Government Accountability Office, the audit, evaluation, and investigative arm of Congress, exists to support Congress in meeting its constitutional responsibilities and to help improve the performance and accountability of the federal government for the American people. GAO examines the use of public funds; evaluates federal programs and policies; and provides analyses, recommendations, and other assistance to help Congress make informed oversight, policy, and funding decisions. GAO's commitment to good government is reflected in its core values of accountability, integrity, and reliability.
Obtaining Copies of GAO Reports and Testimony	The fastest and easiest way to obtain copies of GAO documents at no cost is through GAO's website (www.gao.gov). Each weekday afternoon, GAO posts on its website newly released reports, testimony, and correspondence. To have GAO e-mail you a list of newly posted products, go to www.gao.gov and select "E-mail Updates."
Order by Phone	The price of each GAO publication reflects GAO's actual cost of production and distribution and depends on the number of pages in the publication and whether the publication is printed in color or black and white. Pricing and ordering information is posted on GAO's website, http://www.gao.gov/ordering.htm. Place orders by calling (202) 512-6000, toll free (866) 801-7077, or TDD (202) 512-2537. Orders may be paid for using American Express, Discover Card, MasterCard, Visa, check, or money order. Call for additional information.
Connect with GAO	Connect with GAO on Facebook, Flickr, Twitter, and YouTube. Subscribe to our RSS Feeds or E-mail Updates. Listen to our Podcasts. Visit GAO on the web at www.gao.gov.
To Report Fraud, Waste, and Abuse in Federal Programs	Contact: Website: www.gao.gov/fraudnet/fraudnet.htm E-mail: fraudnet@gao.gov Automated answering system: (800) 424-5454 or (202) 512-7470
Congressional Relations	Katherine Siggerud, Managing Director, siggerudk@gao.gov, (202) 512-4400, U.S. Government Accountability Office, 441 G Street NW, Room 7125, Washington, DC 20548
Public Affairs	Chuck Young, Managing Director, youngc1@gao.gov, (202) 512-4800 U.S. Government Accountability Office, 441 G Street NW, Room 7149 Washington, DC 20548